Still Standing

A True Life Story of Ketrick Jordan

KETRICK JORDAN

NEW SEED
INDUSTRIES
Create, Grow, Disperse

Published by New Seed Industries, LLC
West Bloomfield, MI

Email: newseedllc@gmail.com

Website: www.newseedindustries.com

Still Standing: A True Life Story of Ketrick Jordan
ISBN-13: 978-0-9823640-7-9
ISBN-10: 0-9823640-7-5

Printed in the United States of America

Contents

ACKNOWLEDGEMENTS

I dedicate this book to my sisters and brothers and all the people who are all going through or have been through such a difficult time of a horrific event in the pursuit of their dream of not giving up.

And I would like to thank all of the nurses, doctors and organizations who were there for me in teaching me the skills that I could apply in everyday life.

Chapter One

The Beginning

My name is Ketrick Jordan, and I am the middle child who was born to Beverly Jordan on April 6, 1978. I had two brothers; Bernard Jordan was my older brother and Jamal Jordan was my younger brother. I had two sisters; Demetria Jordan was my older sister and Erica Jordan was my younger sister. I also had a niece named Jasmine Jordan who was my oldest sister's child.

My grandmother, a very strong, caring and supportive lady, took care of me all of my life. My siblings and I, as well as my niece, lived with my grandmother in her four-bedroom home. At that time, I never quite understood or knew why or how we ended up living with my grandmother. But my mother, a good lady, was always there too. My grandmother was a nurse and worked two jobs. So my aunt, who I call "Auntie", at times used to come and spend the night with us. She was the one who kept an eye on us while my grandmother and big sister worked.

My grandmother didn't play when it came time to doing chores; she wanted things cleaned. So we were the kids who had to clean up, unlike my cousins who lived around the corner. They were kind of spoiled. Auntie raised her kids a little different from us.

We didn't have water beds or the new electric big wheel. But my grandmother made sure we had new bikes.

When it was time to go to school, even though my grandmother didn't get off work until six in the morning and didn't make it home until seven, we had to be at the bus stop or else. I remember my cousin coming down every morning around 6:00 a.m., and together we would be laughing while watching the "Three Stooges" on television before we headed off to school. He and my brother Bernard went to the same school. I went to Alta Mesa Elementary School in Dallas, Texas, along with Erica, and my little brother Jamal went to Bishop Heights Elementary School. My big brother Bernard was well-known as a football linebacker. He was a smart guy and tough too. He didn't take anything from anybody. He was a very competitive guy as well.

My oldest sister Demetria was also very smart and a hard working lady. She was on the drill team, the Blue Bells, at Wilmer-Hutchins High School. I think she graduated with top honors being a straight-A student. I remember she had a little Chevy Cheviot stick shift car with a hatchback. On Sundays, she drove like she was flying to church while shifting the gears. And my niece Jasmine, her daughter, was a hand full. She was a big girl and was spoiled rotten. Every time she would see her mother's car leave when my sister went to work, she would scream and cry. She did not want her mother to leave. So, we would ride her around in her stroller to make her stop crying. Now my little sister Erica was a very smart girl. She was tall like me. I remember when her hair had come out after a Jheri curl and perm placed in her hair had gone bad. The kids would tease her about her hair, and I would always take up for her in school. I had to fight a couple of kids on the bus to get them to stop teasing her. Erica loved playing football with us. She would catch the ball and keep on running. I would get mad at her and tackle her so hard, hoping she would stop playing with us.

My little brother Jamal was an introvert type of child who loved playing alone with his toys and hated when it was time to go to the barbershop. I was nicknamed KeeKee. I was a really tall guy with big feet who loved to play football. All I ever played was football. That's all I knew, and I always wanted to become a star. At school, my classwork did not interest me. I knew nothing about doing classwork. It's not because I was not very smart; I just wasn't attentive in class or paid enough attention to complete my lessons. So, I failed the second grade.

Chapter Two

The Influence of Drugs

My grandmother worked all the time, and the only other family members constantly around us were my two uncles, who were always in and out of the house. They were always doing drugs. Drugs were commonly used in our family. It was the environment that we were raised in with drugs and not too much of a father figure in our lives to set a good example. There were times when my uncle stayed at the house with us. When he came, things changed. Both of my uncles were on crack cocaine. And when crack hits the streets in 1988, one of my uncles introduced Bernard to crack and a drug dealer. I wasn't totally sure how true that was, but I knew in my heart that was so because I would see and hear my uncle and Bernard arguing and fighting about money, something which had never occurred prior to him selling drugs. I also saw my uncle steal money out of my sister's purse. One day, I just so happen to walk in the bathroom, and I saw my uncle and his wife smoking crack at my grandmother's house on her toilet. I never saw anything like that before. I was a young guy, and crack was scary when I first saw it. Marijuana was what I was used to seeing.

When my uncle introduced Bernard to crack and the amount of money he would make selling it, Bernard couldn't resist. He liked to look good and wanted those new Magic

Johnson Converse tennis shoes, a new bike, tires, and name-brand clothes. My grandmother was always getting on Bernard after he started coming in late with his eyes red after smoking weed. One late night, I remember him knocking on the windows. We didn't know who it was, but it was him trying to get inside. Erica kept up with Bernard's schedule and would call my grandmother at work to inform her of those times he would sneak in.

Bernard didn't know how much trouble he was making for himself by selling crack and making a lot of money. Once, I listened in on one of his conversations telling someone that his friend got killed somewhere at a bus stop. At that time, I was only 10 years old, so I really didn't know too much. But I felt he had gotten in too deep because as time went by I began to see the fear in his eyes. I knew Bernard was really scared when he started cutting the lawn at night, which was one of the household chores that my grandmother had given him. The drug dealers were shaking him up with all of their threats.

One day Auntie spoke with him about the coach calling her. He said that he had not been to school and was skipping classes. Finally, one night Bernard confessed to my grandmother and told her how afraid he was for his life. Some guys were trying to kill him, and he didn't want to go to school. That scared me really bad. And just a couple of days after he confessed to my grandmother, we start getting threatening phone calls from people we didn't know who spoke with accents. One night, I answered the telephone, and this guy told me he was going to burn my brother's bed down. That really shook Bernard, and I felt his pain. Things had gotten so bad that Bernard was afraid to even leave the house. When we had pizza, he would eat the majority, and then hide the empty pizza boxes behind the deep freezer so my grandmother wouldn't notice how many pizzas he had eaten. And, instead of going out to purchase snacks, he started breaking into my grandmother's locked bedroom when she was at work to take her stash of sodas and chips out of her closet. Eventually, she had to install a bigger lock on her bedroom door to keep Bernard out.

Chapter Three

The Fire

It was the night of September 27, 1988, Auntie and her boyfriend was at the house when Bernard was cutting the lawn late at night and was getting ready to leave. I begged Auntie not to leave because I was scared something would happen to us with all of the threatening calls. She said, "Baby, don't worry about it. Just go in the house, and you'll be okay. Just go to bed because you have school in the morning." But, this night was different. When Bernard finished mowing the lawn, he put up the lawn mower but forgot to put up the gas container. He left it out on our front porch, and I wondered why when it's usually put back in the shed. Early the next morning on September 28, 1988, around two o'clock, Jamal and I were asleep in the room with Demetria and Jasmine since we were now afraid to sleep in our own room. I was awakened by some voices at the front door. I heard Bernard talking to some guys at the door. I asked him who he was arguing with, and for some reason he angrily told me, "Just go back to bed, lay down and don't worry about it!" And as soon as I lay back down, I heard screams coming from Bernard, something I had never heard before. He screamed what we thought was something like, "The gas was on!" When Bernard came back into the house, our house was on fire. Someone had poured the gasoline left out on the front porch throughout our home trapping us in. I tried running to safety. But as soon as I ran out the door, I realized that someone had changed the lock on our gate to trap us in.

Our porch had a burglar-bar gate where when you close it, it latches on its own. The whole house was surrounded by burglary bars. So, there was no way to get out. I tried running from the back room where we slept up the hallway to our living room, but that hallway, our only way out to freedom, was engulfed in flames. We were trapped. To this day, I can still remember what it felt like to feel the heat from the flames and smell the smoke. Demetria tried to break out the windows to get air and ended up cutting her arm from her wrist to her elbow. Bernard yelled, "HELP ME BREAK DOWN GRANDMOTHER'S ROOM DOOR!", but we could not get through the door. We tried everything to break it down, but it wouldn't budge. That was our last and only option for survival and escape. At that point, I could hardly catch my breath to help anyone. Erica was crying saying she couldn't breathe. Everything started falling around us. There was no oxygen, and the heat from the fire was so hot. We were scared. I start helping Erica break out the windows when she said, "I still can't breathe, what should I do?" I told her that we should put our heads underneath the cover, and we did just that. But, it was still hot, and we still couldn't catch our breaths. We tried putting our face and noses to the floor, but it didn't work.

We even tried putting our nose close up to the water in the bathroom to see if that would work, but it did not. I remember telling Erica to put her head up against the burglary bars and try breathing the air from outside. But seconds later, I passed out.

When I passed out I remember going to a place that was unexplainable and felt a power that was indescribable, which changed my life. I never felt so good. I have never seen a place so beautiful. Someone in the brightness of the light was speaking to me, and it felt so good. It left me speechless. I wasn't hungry, nor in pain. I felt real freedom, free from all worries. In that place, I was very happy. The grass was like the Garden of Eden. It was very bright and golden. Then I awoke. When I awoke, I immediately saw lights. I was lying on the cold ground with my whole body feeling numb and in pain. Then, I heard the voice of a firefighter screaming, "Hey, hey! We got one alive!" And in the midst of all the lights and me lying on the ground, I looked up and saw Auntie who always wore this big red t-shirt when she went to bed at night. Then I knew this wasn't a dream. This really did happen, and it felt like I was in hell because I was back to all of the pain, heartache and evil. As the firefighters picked me up onto the gurney to take me away, I caught a glimpse of Jamal lying on his side and the firefighters flipping him over to do CPR. I asked about my little brother with my voice now a raspy whisper caused by smoke inhalation but never got a response.

One firefighter placed a blanket on me while another one started spreading cream on my arm and badly burned legs. I told them I was thirsty but was told we were almost at the hospital. That's when I looked down at my legs and saw how badly burned they were; I could actually see the bone.

Chapter Four

The Hospital

My mother and my cousin were already at the hospital when we arrived. I told my mother that I was really thirsty and needed some water. As she tried to hand me a cup of water, the doctor knocked the cup out of her hand and said, "You would kill him with that." We didn't know at that time, but drinking any fluids could increase the chances of causing more harm to your airways. In the emergency room, the doctor cut off my now black and soot-stained underwear. I was in so much pain! The fingers on my left hand were so badly burned, that my fingertips were hanging off from the first knuckle just below the fingernail. Then the doctor said, "Mr. Jordan, we have to amputate both of your legs above the knee in order for you to survive." That was the last thing I remembered before losing my legs.

I don't know how long I stayed in a coma or actually how many times I died or how long I was on a breathing machine. But when I awoke, the first person I saw was Auntie, who was pregnant at the time with my little cousin. She was wearing a hospital gown, which reminded me that I was in the hospital. Initially, when I first saw Auntie I was happy, and I thought I was going to be able to go home. But sadly, that was not going to happen as I immediately realized after looking down at my legs that they were actually gone.

As I looked around my room, hanging to the left side of my bed was a unit of blood and all types of IVs and I had a little red dot placed on my finger. When I tried to speak I couldn't. Auntie told me to write down what I wanted to say. I asked about my sisters and brothers. She said, "KeeKee baby, don't worry about that right now." Immediately, I felt that they were no longer alive. When Auntie and my grandmother would come to visit me, I would continually ask them, "Where are my sisters and brothers?" They would give me the same response as before until one day as I watched television, I saw pictures of my family members being displayed as the anchor person gave a news update of our house bombing and stated that they were deceased.

Chapter Five

The Physical Healing Process

The process of getting my burns and skin grafts scrubbed was the most excruciating, unimaginable pain I ever felt. There would be screams from little babies and little children coming from the hallway. You would think that they were crying about the loss of loved ones, but those were screams from other survivors having their burns scrubbed. It hurt so bad I thought I was not going to be able to survive this process or even get to go home. Every day, and sometimes twice a day, I had to endure the seemingly endless pain of having my burns scrubbed in the whirlpool and seeing the residue of my blood left behind. I was known at Parkland Memorial Hospital in Dallas, Texas, for my frequent crying and screaming. They would frequently have to switch my nurse because of it until one day I was assigned a nurse named Jack who had to scrub my burns. He told me, "I'm not going to be your nurse anymore because I just can't take this. This is just too much for me." I really liked Jack because he would not rip the bandages off of me. He would just place me in the whirlpool, let me relax and allow the bandages to soak off. So, when Jack left, I realized my screams were making even the good nurses leave. So I decided to stop screaming out as bad. Then there was a woman named "Big Shirley" who would always tell me, "No pain and no gain." I never understood what that meant until I heard the song by Betty Wright, "No Pain, No Gain," and that stuck with me forever. My body was ravaged with pain. I had pain from having fourth-degree burns on my hand, fingers, back, buttocks and also severe pain on my stubs. The pain was something I had to get used to, or mentally it felt like I wasn't going to make it. My body had to endure skin grafts that were then placed under heat lamps, blood transfusions, a tracheal that was inserted in my esophagus to help me breathe, and a feeding tube that was inserted for me to be able to eat. At one point, I only weighed between 40 and 50 pounds.

My stay at this hospital was about two to three months. I kept asking myself, "How did I get here?" I knew that I was on the road to recovery. However, mentally and physically it was very painful. It's hard lying in a hospital bed when you constantly see people, nurses, children and their families going home, and I had to stay and endure the pain of my burns. There were times when my grandmother would visit me, and I didn't want to see her. She would be talking to me, and I wouldn't acknowledge or even look at her all because I felt she, my mom and Auntie left us there to die in that fire. Although, there were many more times I felt good about seeing them coming and being there with me. My grandmother would rub my head when she would come to see me in the hospital and tell me that I'm here for a reason and that she loved me. Those great words of encouragement gave me the strength to move forward.

One goal of mine was to be transferred from the intensive care unit to the outpatient side of the hospital, but it was a process. It took me a while to eat regular foods; usually, I would just suck on a towel and eat a lot of popsicles to try to increase my weight. Thankfully, I was able to get rid of my feeding tube and began eating regular foods, which helped increase my weight due in part from the encouragement and the multiple visits from the chaplain of Parkland Memorial Hospital and the nurses of the burn unit. Unfortunately, even with all of the support, the mental pain of this whole ordeal was still hard for me to keep up with my eating. So, they had to place me back on a feeding tube, and this delayed the process of me being an outpatient. But with prayer, plenty more words of encouragement, good people coming to see me, and good nurses to assist me, I got that feeding tube removed once again. To help restore the use of my arm, a nurse would come and assist me in extending my arm to touch the hanging balloon that was placed above my bed to stretch the severely burned skin underneath my armpit, which was very painful and agonizing. But, this was what I had to do to make my arm better. After a month or two in the intensive care unit, I was finally able to get the breathing tubes taken out of my nose. It was comforting to hear the doctor say that I could be transferred over to the outpatient side of the hospital since I was able to talk, and that made me feel great. Even though I was able to speak, the tracheal was still in my throat to help with my breathing.

Another milestone I had to accomplish was for me to get the catheter removed. Being on the outpatient side of the hospital, I still had to endure the continuous pain of the whirlpool baths, them scrubbing my burns and me feeling the staples that were in my back and on my buttocks. The fingers on my left hand were still hanging off, and everything still was very painful. But I was grateful to be out of the intensive care unit. The day arrived when they removed my tracheal. I felt like I was at the barbershop when a cloth is placed around your neck and you are waiting to have your hair cut. I asked the nurse if I should hold something. She replied, "No," and slowly proceeded to take out the tracheal. After completing the procedure, she placed a piece of gauze over the hole and said in time the hole would heal and close up. And it did, but I was left with a scar. The last hurdle for me being able to go home was to get the folding catheter removed. That day finally came and what a painful experience it was. It's something that I never want to go through again. After a long time, the day that I had been waiting for had arrived; I was able to go home. My mother was there along with my grandmother. Now, instead of constantly watching others out of the window going home, I felt the excitement because it was my turn. It was as if a world I was unfamiliar with was being made a reality. There were gifts, get-well wishes and even the news media was present taking pictures of me all while telling me to get well.

Chapter Six

Adjusting to Home Life

Adjusting to my new way of life at my grandmother's home was really difficult. I was excited to be home, but I didn't know all the adjustments I would need to make in order to learn how to get around and to take care of myself now that I had disabilities. I couldn't even crawl. I was familiar with using the bed urinal at the hospital, but going to the bathroom and just getting around at home were challenging. At least at the hospital, the doors were wider than the ones in my home. Someone had given my grandmother a bell for me to ring when I needed assistance. She would bring me my food, run my bath water and even change my dressings on the burn wounds. Auntie would come and help out a lot too. But at night, it was hard to sleep. I had restless, lonely nights. When I would fall asleep, I would have nightmares about the fire and wake up screaming. It was really a hard time for me and my grandmother as she had to get up for work in the morning, and my screams would wake her disturbing her sleep. Then one night, my grandmother, not sure of how I would feel, hesitantly asked me if I wanted to go spend some time with my mother. My poor mother used drugs to cope with her losses, but I wanted to go spend some time with her. So I went.

After being at my mother's home, I stopped using the bell to ring for assistance. Initially, it was okay. But after a while, my mother helped me understand the need for starting to take care of myself. Eventually, I went back to my grandmother's home and took the initiative to start caring for myself. I wanted to learn to crawl, and my grandmother got me a gadget that was used to move furniture to assist me. It helped me, but it was difficult since my left hand was still very tender, and my fingers still hung loosely from my hand. I really needed both hands to help me with the gadget. So I made a decision. I told my grandmother that at my next doctor's visit, I wanted him to amputate my three hanging fingers.

Chapter Seven

Amputation of My Fingers

My doctors initially wanted to see if the bone that was sticking out of my hand would help to regroup the fingers. But that didn't happen, and the constant changing of the dressing on my hand at therapy twice a week was always such excruciating pain. I thought by amputating my fingers it would help a lot in moving around without having loosely hanging fingers getting in the way, and it would also relieve the pain of redressing. Anything at that point to avoid the pain I was experiencing was alright with me. So, the doctors amputated my fingers. Now, I could get from the floor to the chair and back down and crawl around the house as well as get to the toilet from the floor and in and out of bed. It's amazing how you can learn to do things differently when you make up your mind to do it. The encouragement and support of others around me helped fuel my drive to live and to keep going so that I could become more independent and feel better about myself.

Chapter Eight

Adjusting to Society

The hardest thing about recovery was reconnecting with my peers. But I knew in order to continue the stages of healing I had to get back out into society. There would be endless questions like, "What happened to your legs? Why does your skin look like that? What's wrong with your hand? Why are you in a wheelchair?" I knew the questions would come with me being a double amputee having both legs cut off above my knees and with fourth-degree burns over 65 percent of my body. It was definitely hard for me dealing with all the questions and still trying out my new skills to maneuver in my wheelchair, which at times fell backward while I tried to pop wheelies. One day while going to the grocery store with my grandmother, some kids in the aisle looked and said, "Mom he has no legs." That was heartbreaking to me. I didn't think people looked at others like that. Instead, it would have been easier if the kids had asked me what happened. With me being 11 or 12 years old and already very conscious of my body image, that was really hurtful to hear.

Once, my doctor recommended chlorine water to help heal my burns. So my grandmother, Auntie, my uncle, his lady friend and I went swimming in our community pool. Everyone got in the pool. But when I got in, the people got out just because of how my skin looked. That taught me right then that people will judge you by the way you look without even knowing what you went through. I didn't ask to wake up one day without legs and consequently be judged unfairly by others. That was the second hardest thing I had to endure. But, I am thankful for my grandmother's encouragement and her telling me to forget those people for they didn't know what I had been through and for my cousins being there for me to speak up and tell people politely to not say certain things or to not ask questions. Emotionally dealing with people who pointed, stared and commented on my looks made me self-conscience. I got to a point where I would try to hide parts of my body. My arm was really bright pink from healing. So I covered it with a bandana. And even now at times, depending on the situation, it can still be difficult. I made new friends and did a lot of local news interviews, but the adjustment was still hard. I didn't know how to feel being recently discharged from the hospital and wanting to be with my old friends but being unable to since we relocated to a different part of the city to live after the fire.

Chapter Nine

Getting my Prosthetics

When I entered Scottish Wright Hospital, the hospital and staff chosen to help me walk again, it was such a great atmosphere. I never thought I would see so many people and children like me. Not because they were burned, but because they were amputees. Some were in way worse conditions than I was, and that greatly inspired me to go on. Once I got there, it changed a lot of broken pieces in my life. I met an extraordinary guy named Dr. Don Cummings. He was the director over prosthetics and one of the ones responsible for getting me up and teaching me how to walk again. He designed my prosthetics according to my height, my shoe size and even by the color that I chose. When I met him, he had two prosthetic legs, which was crazy to me because he was walking normally. You would never know he'd lost both of his legs. He was a double amputee below the knees, unlike me who had no knees, but still was an inspiration for me to want to walk again. This part of the process was fun for me because I got to control how my legs looked. So, I picked a black metallic background and Tasmanian Devil in a spin motion with a football since I always wanted to be a professional football player. That was crazy because the first one to have those types of legs was the Tasmanian Devil. I wanted something different because I was different. I was looked at differently, and I was in the mindset of having something different. My feet were painted red with black toenails, and that was pretty awesome. But getting to walk on those was very hard for me. My stumps would break out and bleed from the pressure applied to them from walking. But, I had to toughen them up for me to walk with the prosthetics. I once told my nurse that I couldn't do it. She told me, "KeeKee, you have to get up and walk the halls on your legs to make them tough, or else you will not be able to accomplish your goal of wanting to walk again. Didn't you say you wanted to jump off the curb?" That made me laugh, and I responded, "Yeah, I did". It was a difficult process getting fitted for my prosthetics, and it even amazed my doctors who had never seen a person that badly scarred walking on prosthetics. When I started walking again, I remember thinking, "Wow, I'm part of the norm. I'm part of society. I'm coming back!"

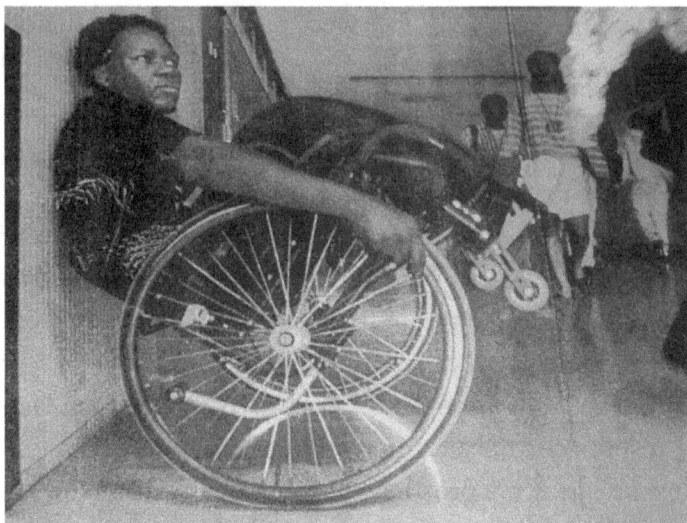

Ketrick at school in his wheelchair. (Dallas Morning News photo)

Chapter Ten

Time for School

It was time for me to go back to school, but my grandmother and I felt uncomfortable with me still having to change my bandages twice a week. And, I was still adjusting to how people looked at me and being out into society again. So, my grandmother decided to put me in an all-black, Catholic private school named St. Anthony where the environment was more controlled than that of a public school. Being the only guy in the school who was considered different, it was a new emotional experience for me. My cousin Reggie went to the same school.

So that made me feel a little comfort as I knew he would protect me. If at any given moment someone tried talking about me or bullying me, I knew he would be there to defend me. So that relieved a lot of the jitters, nervousness and embarrassment that I was feeling. But as soon as the first day of school came, I immediately became shy because the news media was at the school asking questions.

Initially, things were going well as I got settled into school. I was wearing my uniform and walking on my artificial legs with the aid of two crutches, the type that goes around your elbow. But then things started to change, and the people in my class started bullying me. I knew these things were going to happen and that I would just have to learn how to deal with it, especially since I couldn't balance myself or stand without support to even try to fight. But I had to figure something out fast in order to keep people from eating me alive. Some days my feelings would really get hurt when my cousin and his new friends would make jokes, do pranks or laugh at me. And to make matters worse, I had a big, long desk with a cushioned teacher-type chair instead of a regular desk like the other students because of my burned buttock. Once during break time, I was returning from the restroom when some guys started laughing. I didn't know why until one day my cousin told me they had put pins under my seat cushion because he told them that I would not be able to feel it. I questioned my cousin as to why he would do that to me. To this day, the memory of it still hurts.

When those horrible things were happening to me, it was as if a callous had been placed over my heart when I realized that I had no one to defend me. Surely my cousin loved me, but I knew if my brothers and sisters were alive, they would not have intentionally helped others hurt me.

Another time, some students poured water on the floor and stood in the hallway waiting for me. As soon as I entered the classroom, they laughed as they watched me slip and fall. Mentally, I wasn't prepared for school, but my grandmother wanted me to start practicing my independence, something I did not know at the time. Nevertheless, it was really hard for me. It was so difficult adjusting that I had to go to summer school to pass my fifth-grade year since I failed it. But that was my turning point. Overall going to school was good for me because incidents like those mentally helped toughen me up. I was put in a position where it made me have to use my mind since being physically capable was not an option. I realized that I had to strategize to conquer those things and pay close attention to detail. It was also my first time experiencing how one's peers really view you when you have a different ability. School also taught me that sometimes you will feel left out and nobody will be there to help you. I made every effort to be considered part of "the norm" as I never labeled myself as handicapped or disabled. I considered those words as something referring to a computer. In my mind, I viewed a handicapped person as being someone with their hand out asking for money.

Well, I did not ask anyone for help. And, thanks to my grandmother and the rest of my family for being supportive of the various camps that I attended, the skills that I learned made me ready to face society. When I felt like I didn't want to live anymore because of the way I looked or I wasn't able to do the things I always wanted to do like play football, I was reminded that physically I could do things. However, it would just take some time to accomplish them. I was good at football, and sports were always a major thing in my life before the fire. Dealing with not being able to play sports was something quite different. It was in my sixth-grade year, I overcame the loneliness. It helped that I was able to sit at a regular desk. I never thought of myself as being a smart person up until now. I was learning how to do my best in reading, writing, and understanding the Bible as well as learning things that other people didn't know that I was learning like being able to climb a couple of steps to get inside the church building, playing kickball and volleyball with my classmates, as well as participating in other activities besides football. It was a great gift, but it was also very hard for me.

Chapter Eleven

Middle School

After feeling more confident and safe enough, my grandmother enrolled me in Fred F. Florence Middle School, my neighborhood public middle school. There were gangs, but I used to live in the "hood". I came from the "hood," which was more like a community and not like a ghetto. I knew about that type of environment, so I maneuvered like a chameleon. I no longer had to wear uniforms, but I knew how to straddle the fence to blend in and still stay out of the way. In my community, great emphasis was placed on looking good. So the only way I knew how to fit in was to dress well in brand-named clothes like K-Swiss, Guess, Levi, and Karl Kani. And it was during this time that the bullying slowed down but not the pranks. The pranks continued, I guess, because people just wanted to do things.

Being a teenager, I had to know who I was. My grandmother wanted me to know who I was. So, by going to various camps and staying active, something I knew I had to do, I learned more about myself and how to do things differently, especially when people tended to stare if certain things were not done properly. Scottish Wright Hospital connected me to a lot of different camp programs when I was in middle school. We use to take trips, and it helped build my confidence. I learned many things at these camps that included swimming, arts and crafts. Once, I went to this beautiful place in Colorado where they taught me the art of horseback riding and the importance of allowing the horse to know the rider. They taught us how to start a fire. We were all in wheelchairs. Another guy taught me how to drive a little hatchback, stick shift car up in the mountains. It was funny because there was no place to drive the car. The experience left me speechless. This showed me that there are good, regular, normal people in the world. Volunteers put in a lot of time and effort to make those enrolled at camp feel comfortable and they tried to bring us back to somewhat of a place of normality, something we thought would never happen again. Sometimes we felt like castaways, but because the volunteers were on our side and willing to help see us through, we felt better. The volunteers also taught us how to pack our things and to bring only the essential items needed to help us since some of us were physically sicker than others. But those who were sick still went camping. They would just have medical nurses to help comfort them. We experienced a lot by being out in the woods. We heard the sounds of the wolves and the screeching of the crickets. We washed our plates in the running Colorado River Springs. We learned how to fish and how to canoe. We even learned how to flip the canoe back over if it overturned; imagine people with no legs and no arms learning how to flip canoes. But, we worked as a team, and that taught us teamwork.

There was another great camp that my grandmother placed me in that was recommended by the Parkland Burn

Center. That was my first time at a burn camp. I was so thrilled and excited to be around people just like me. They let us write our names on the concrete, something they did with every group that had been through the camp. Some people were so badly burned that they had to wear masks on their faces to keep their skin from getting puffy and then falling flat. I saw people who were weak, just like I used to be, who needed us stronger ones to assist them. The camp was divided into groups. I was in the older group with both boys and girls. Some were weaker than others. Those of us who were stronger had to show the others, and not just with mere words but through our actions, how to build their confidence. For example, one girl was afraid to jump into the water that had a missing leg as it had been amputated due to severe burns. I dove into the pool and swam to her. I told her that she can do it because I did it, and I was missing both of my legs. Scottish Wright Hospital also offered a winter camp for a ski trip. This was one sport I really loved. Downhill skiing was one of the best sports I could ever experience. I used one regular size ski underneath the seat and two little skis, which is used for guiding the ski. This is called a mono-ski that is used by paralyzed or amputee persons. I loved mono skiing. I am probably the only one from my hometown to be able to do blue and black diamonds and go down moguls. No one can downplay my experience of learning how to ski as a double amputee above the knees.

Life for me was like a person being imprisoned who

knows they will never get out. I discovered if you set your mind as though you're in prison, you will die. And even though that's how I felt, I refused to have that mindset as being handicapped or disabled. I was supposed to be in a special class, but I went to one of the parent-teacher conferences and told them that this made me feel uncomfortable. Special classes made me feel as if I was disabled or handicapped, and I wanted to be around regular people or the people who they said were regular, even though the regular people also had problems. They agreed and let me stay in the regular classes. I wanted to be different. I knew there were certain things I couldn't do, but that is where the different camps helped. There were always people at the camps who had missing limbs, like a leg, an arm or maybe two arms, and still kept going. Middle school ended up being like a breath of fresh air for me. I sang and participated in little singing events in class. One year in middle school, I even won a first place trophy in a dance competition for doing wheelies in my wheelchair.

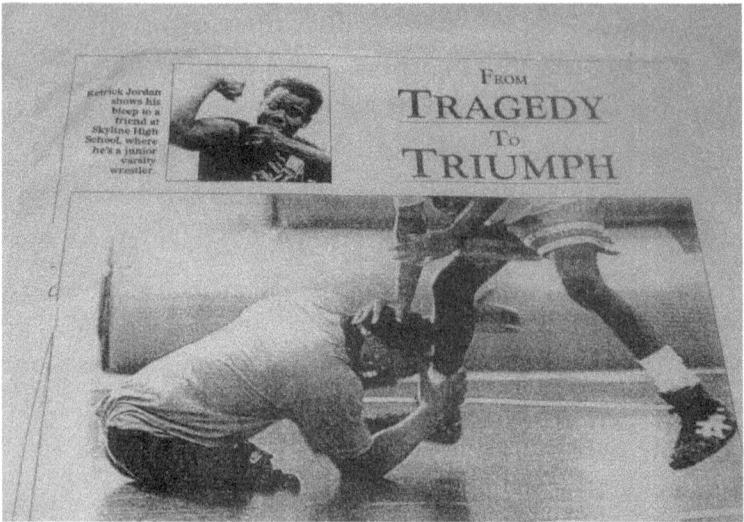

Ketrick a junior varsity wrestler for Skyline High School. (Dallas Morning News photo)

Chapter Twelve

High School

Entering my adolescence years, I wanted different things. This was mainly due to the camps and the support of my family who taught me how to love myself and how to be comfortable with just being me, where before I used to be afraid of who I was. I knew that there were people who really loved me. So, I put aside wanting to hide the way I looked. I stopped wrapping my arms and became educated not only about school but about colognes as well as clothing styles. I was on my game. High school was different from middle school. So I had to figure out how I could fit in again, and I decided it'd be through my style. My style included the clothes that I dressed in, my hair which was long and had finger waves and being buff with muscles from playing sports. I wore my artificial legs, and at times I got around in my wheelchair to get to some of my classes that were located outside in another building because the school was so big. Most people didn't know that I had artificial legs, except those who lived in my neighborhood, my girlfriend at that time and those who went to my school. I loved school. I loved science, biology, English and writing classes. I didn't like math so much, but I did okay in the class. Everything else was smooth sailing for me. I would get up early in the morning and arrive before anyone else to go to the student center to do my homework. Being in high school, I had a lot of ambition. I felt grown; especially considering the things I had previously experienced and learned from my uncles and other people in my family. I considered myself old at heart. There is nothing that I would hear or be told that would surprise me.

It was during my first year at Skyline Magnet High School in Dallas, Texas, where I met my good friend Chad. He was really a great friend. When I entered high school, I thought, "Wow!" My mind was on the girls, sports and figuring out how I could fit in. My counselor enrolled me in an elective cooking and sewing class because I was in a wheelchair. I thought to myself, "Here I go again. Please put me in a class with the normal students." So I requested a meeting with my counselor. The first thing he said was, "I hear you have a problem with your classes." To which I replied, "Yes sir". And he asked, "What's the problem? I thought you liked your classes?" I told him I did, but I wanted to be involved in sports. He suggested a swimming class. I told him that I already knew how to swim. He proceeded to name other sports like baseball and football. I said that I was not interested in those sports either. But when he mentioned wrestling, I said, "Wrestling? You mean like when they say, 'One, two and three. You're out.'?" He said, "Yes, wrestling." I immediately replied, "Boom, put me in coach." When I first started wrestling, everyone would look at me like, "Wow. This guy wants to wrestle, and we have to wrestle him? But we don't want to hurt him." I'm what they saw as handicapped. That was their first impression of me not knowing that I was a force to be reckoned with.

My main focus at school was being the best at whatever I did. I was really getting into wrestling. It surprised a lot of people when I came to practice without my prosthetic legs. So Coach Karl's wife made me singlet tights so that I could cover up my stumps. They had little grip pads on them. That was special, and I felt like I was the man. I had come such a long way, and I couldn't be stopped. I became one of the most popular people at school because I was on the wrestling team. People were always going to the football and basketball games. But now, the people I spoke to every day at school, who didn't know I had artificial legs, wanted to see for themselves, especially since I had been on the news. When I wrestled, the matches were packed events. It was difficult for me to crawl out onto the mats because I knew people were watching me for being a double amputee. But when I heard the people shouting my name on both sides, it was crazy. I would hear the opposing team rooting for me to beat their players. I never saw anything like that before. At one point, I was the fastest in the state of Texas on takedowns, I could bench 200 pounds while only weighing 112 pounds and I was one of the best junior varsity wrestlers. I never felt being a wrestler and being showcased on television was a big deal. Rather, I would have felt better if I had been recognized as a wrestler who wasn't allowing what he's been through to make him feel down because I chose not to be silent. I spoke up to my counselor for not wanting to be singled out. I didn't think that I was doing all that much. After surviving being burned and coming out of the hospital, that was the biggest deal of my life.

It was also during this time that I got involved in other activities, such as public speaking after meeting Bill Demby, a great friend of mine who lost both of his legs below the knees in Vietnam when he stepped onto a mine. Bill had a commercial sponsored by DuPont and after Bill would shoot his commercials, he would go play basketball with other guys who had both of their legs. When he went up for a shot, he would get blocked and pushed down on his prosthesis. Then the guys, noticing his artificial legs, would give him a helping hand back up. This inspired me to go on. Bill took me out on a couple of his events where he did motivational speaking, and the words he spoke describing what he had been through showed me that I could encourage others to do the same. I would tell others my story, explain why I kept a smile on my face and why I carried on as I did. This opportunity allowed me to be a special guest at Disney World in Orlando, Florida, where I was able to learn about the sea life, meet Mickey and Minnie Mouse, go to the Epcot Center and meet many different people.

Ketrick's Essence Award (Dallas Morning News photo)

Chapter Thirteen

My Essence Award

It was very surprising to be contacted and informed that I was nominated for an Essence Award. At the time, I didn't even know what an Essence Award was. My grandmother explained to me that Jet and Essence magazines had awards for people who inspired others. It really excited me to know what the award stood for, especially after realizing the definition of essence is the makeup of something. To know that I was being recognized for the makeup of a person of color deeply touched me. I won the award! When I got the call for my Essence Award, it really hurt and excited me at the same time. My award stated,

"The 1996 Essence Award presented to Ketrick Jordan for challenging, inspiring and enlightening others with your resilient message of hope and love." This inspired me in ways I couldn't believe, and I felt like one of the richest, most famous people in the world. The things I had accomplished being disabled I did for myself. This award also hurt me because it reminded me of my great friend Bill Demby, who I had lost contact with but used to accompany on his speaking engagements. I would have loved to share this experience with him, considering it was his influence which brought me this far. That experience also afforded me the opportunity to meet Oprah Winfrey when I was a special guest at a dinner event where they discovered Ramses' tomb. I received one of fifty of his gold pieces. Oprah Winfrey extended an invitation for me to share my story, but I was unable to because of the circumstances surrounding the case. The police were still investigating the fire at my home and there was still too much circumstantial evidence that had not been proven or explained. Even though I was unable to go to her show, she still sent me some souvenir shirts and coffee cups.

EPILOGUE

In this world, you have to look at someone who gives you the strength to achieve something difficult. And when you find that someone, grab hold of their rope and climb it. My family's love and support and the people who came into my life at such a vulnerable time gave me the strength and ambition to achieve what I have and continue to do so for the goals that I am still trying to achieve. For anybody who has been through something as devastating as I, I urge you to put yourself in various camp programs. They really will help you, and if it wasn't for these camp programs, I don't know where I would be today. It showed me life continues going on, and I'm pretty good. There are people in worse conditions, and I saw it for myself. It is beneficial and imperative that you surround yourself with people of many different disabilities before you try to make it on your own.

I thank the Lord, for when he saved my life, he instilled in my heart and my soul the understanding of what pain is for every man and woman of the world. I know the strength and courage it takes to survive from being the only one left from the fire and just having that last memory, which will always be in that grey area of my mind, of my sisters, brothers and niece screaming and crying out for help. But yet and still, it was something about that place I went to that was so beautiful that instilled in me not to give up but to keep going.

That experienced has changed the way I think, how I view things, my perception of people, my lifestyle, and my beliefs. It changed my whole life in just a few seconds. Never would I forget a place so unimaginable.

You may ask, "How did I make it through the pain and heartache?" God, it's because He alone can help you to cope with the pain of loss. The horrible memories remain, but He can help you even in that. When you have been stripped of everything and have lost so much, knowing that you can't get it back, and you come out of it with missing body limbs or family members, it makes you want to keep living. It gives you strength because when you were at your lowest point and you come up from there, it's amazing! It's an unexplainable gift from God. I had to first learn that I have to always believe in myself and love me before I could believe in anything else. You must believe in yourself. That was the only way I was able to make it through. Understand this life is more mental than it is physical. I had to learn that and a lot of other things, such as how people label or judge others instead of looking at them for who they are. Or, how certain people love you just for who you are. Uniqueness makes us who we are, and we didn't come into this world by ourselves. So we can't do this by ourselves. To this day, it still brings tears to my eyes when I look in the mirror. I realize that I am a strong individual, an example that is needed in the world and someone who understands that there is a difference between having a different ability and being handicapped.

When you have been in the darkness, the darkness soon teaches you that you can be of useful. Then, you become more understanding and agreeable to the darkness. You become accustomed to it. When I was in the darkness, I learned the darkness, and I learned not to be afraid. But when I finally came home and saw the light, I learned to appreciate the light better than I would if this had never happened to me. With fourth-degree burns on both of my stumps, one all over the left and on my right just underneath the bottom, it wasn't easy getting to the top. But thank God I did it! Camps made the difference for me. And with that discovery, I felt the overwhelming need to tell my testimony, especially living in a world of such unrest, fighting, violence and hatred.

I am grateful for being here. I want to inspire others and show people that if you are living productive lives and your brain still works, you are not disabled. You have a different ability. And that doesn't mean you can't do it, you just learn to do it a different way. Life is such a wonderful journey. It is filled with both beautiful and hurtful things. Life is a blessing and we are all here for a reason. So don't give up. Don't let time pass you by and don't look at life like it is not worth living. Get up and take action now because someone is in dire need of you! I really hope this book can touch someone and give them a reason to live because someone gave me a reason to live. Someone gave me a reason to carry on, and I want to be able to inspire others to do the same. I am still standing because of God's never-ending mercy, strength and grace. And, I never gave up.

About the Author

Ketrick Jordan is the proud father of a daughter, Maya Jordan, whom he loves dearly. He has an associate degree in criminal justice from Remington College in Dallas, Texas, where he received recognition for starting the Victims Impact Panel from the Criminal Justice Club in 2011.

Ketrick volunteers his time by engaging in motivational speaking to trouble teens at alternative schools, churches, and, at times, the Juvenile Justice Center. Additionally, he sets up water stations for the Susan G. Komen's Race for the Cure.

Ketrick desires to start his own organization to provide resources and accessible housing for individuals with different abilities. Meanwhile, his focus is to inspire youth and adults with disabilities or different abilities who have been affected by either criminal activity or bad decisions to know that through all the pain and physical limitations, life still can be lived to the fullest through perseverance.

NEW SEED
INDUSTRIES
Create. Grow. Disperse

Published by New Seed Industries, LLC
West Bloomfield, MI

Email: newseedllc@gmail.com

Website: www.newseedindustries.com

www.ingramcontent.com/pod-product-compliance
Lightning Source LLC
Chambersburg PA
CBHW060056050426
42448CB00011B/2493